Famous & Fun Duets

6 Duets for One Piano, Four Hands

Carol Matz

Famous & Fun Duets, Book 4, contains carefully selected familiar songs and timeless masterworks of the great composers. The duets are arranged in equal parts for early intermediate pianists, and are written for one piano, four hands. For easier reading, each part is written using both treble and bass clefs, with directions for the *primo* to play up an octave and the *secondo* down an octave. Additionally, the melody often shifts between *primo* and *secondo,* creating interesting parts for both players. Students are sure to enjoy their experience with these fun duets!

Carol Matz

Alfred Music Publishing Co., Inc.
P.O. Box 10003
Van Nuys, CA 91410-0003
alfred.com

ISBN-10: 0-7390-7652-3
ISBN-13: 978-0-7390-7652-1

Flower Duet

(from the opera *Lakmé*)

Secondo

Léo Delibes
Arranged by Carol Matz

Flower Duet

(from the opera *Lakmé*)

Primo

Léo Delibes
Arranged by Carol Matz

Moderately

Play both hands one octave higher

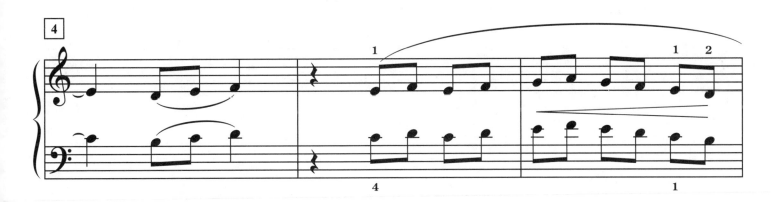

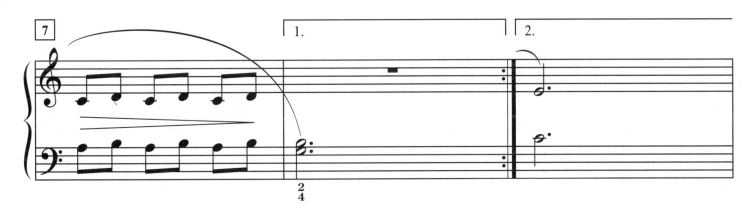

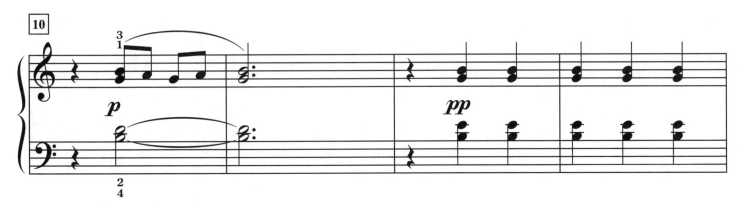

Secondo

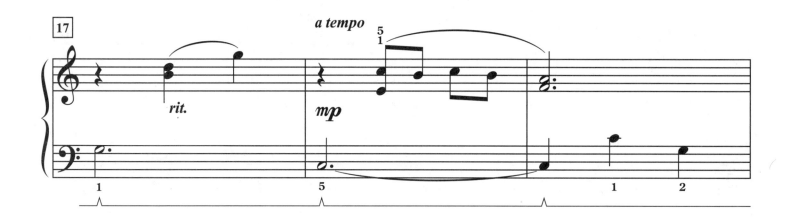

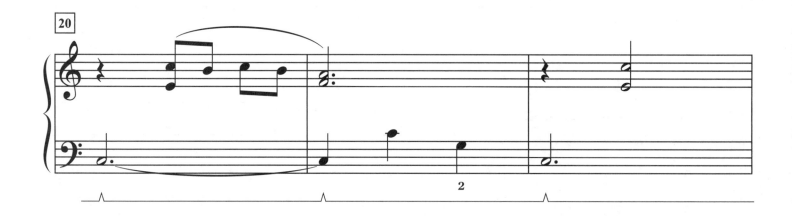

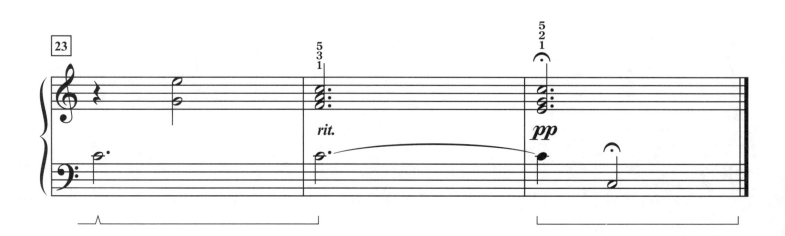

Primo

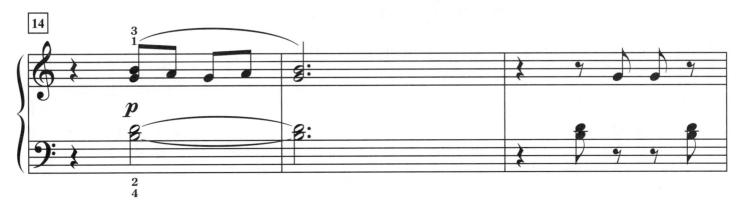

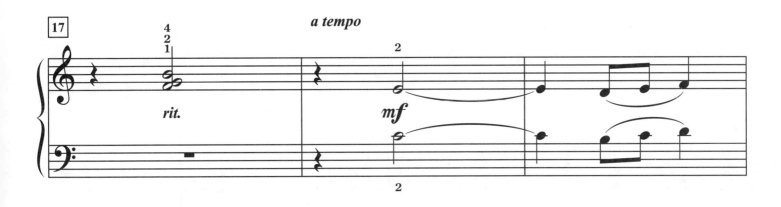

Skaters Waltz

Secondo

Emil Waldteufel
Arranged by Carol Matz

Skaters Waltz

Primo

Emil Waldteufel
Arranged by Carol Matz

Secondo

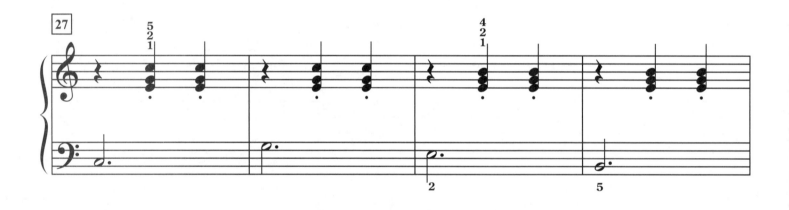

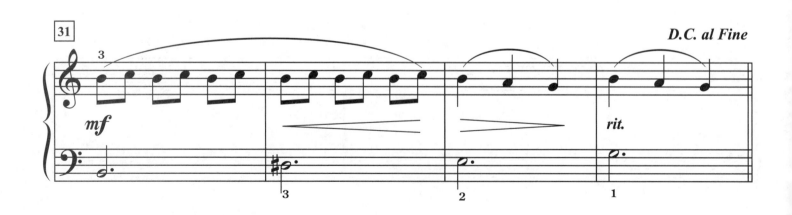

Primo

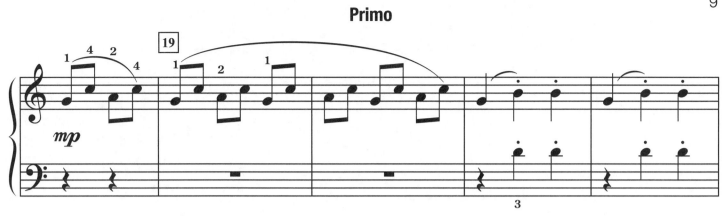

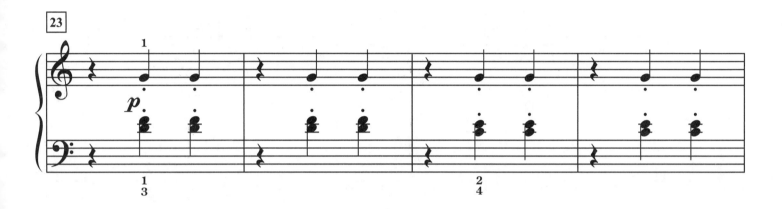

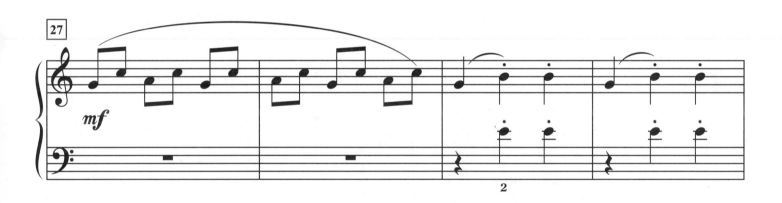

D.C. al Fine

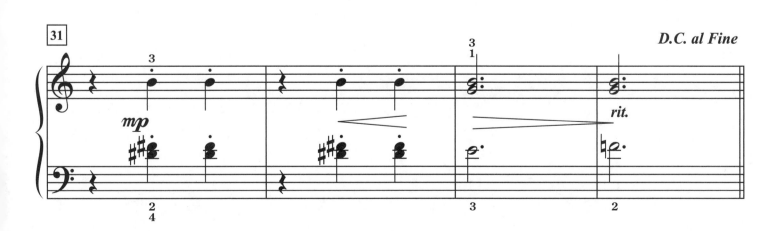

Wedding Tarantella

Secondo

Traditional Italian Dance
Arranged by Carol Matz

Lively

Play both hands one octave lower

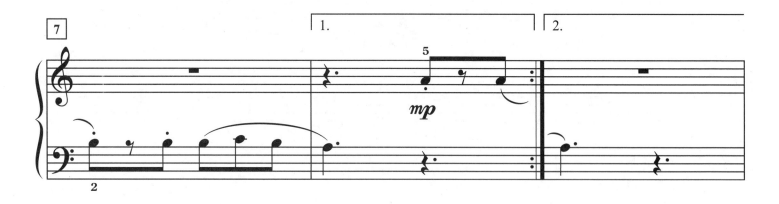

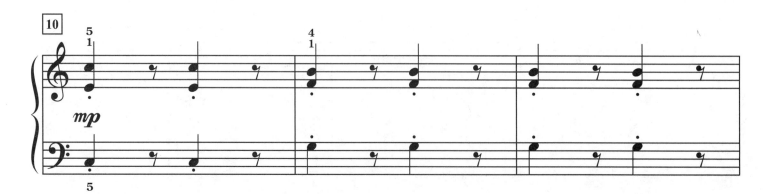

Wedding Tarantella

Primo

Traditional Italian Dance
Arranged by Carol Matz

Lively

Play both hands one octave higher

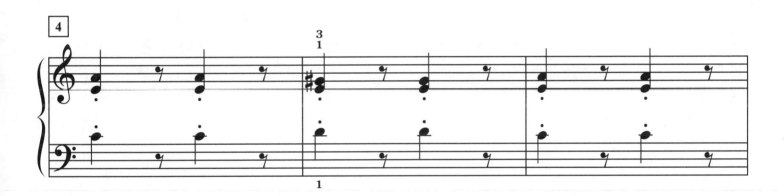

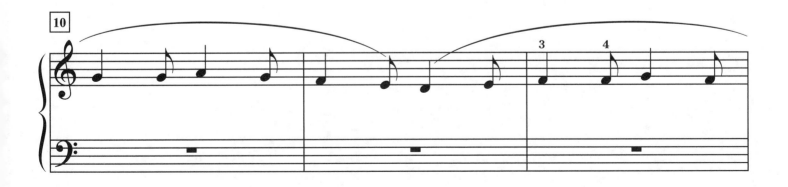

Secondo

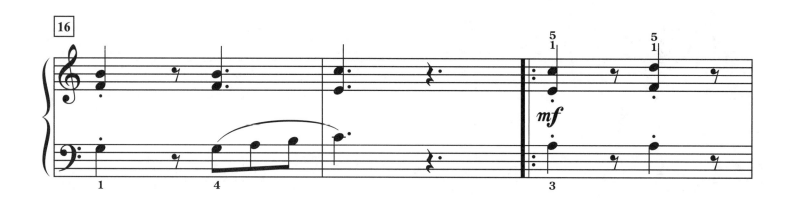

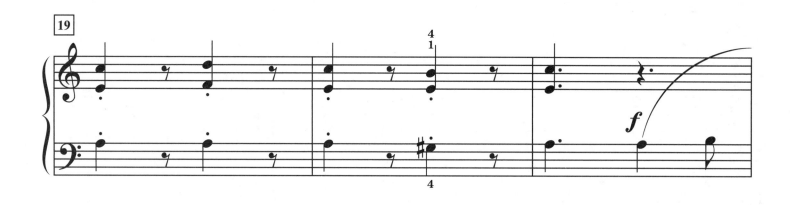

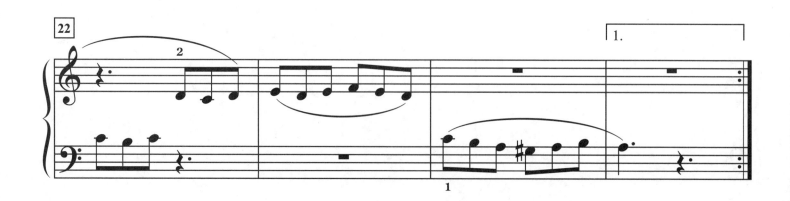

Primo

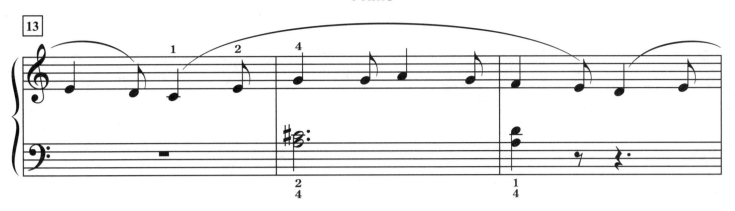

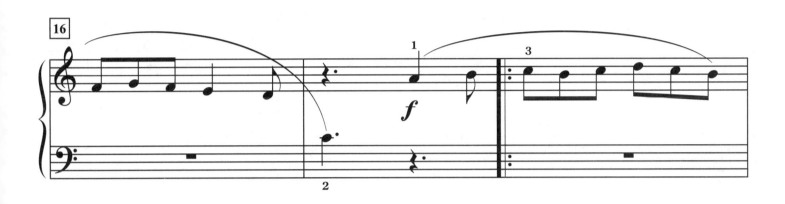

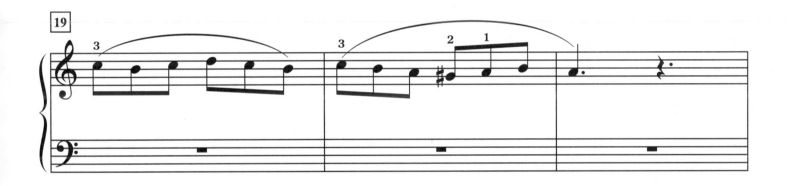

Secondo

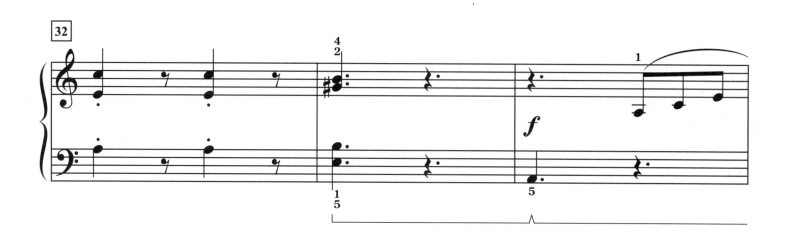

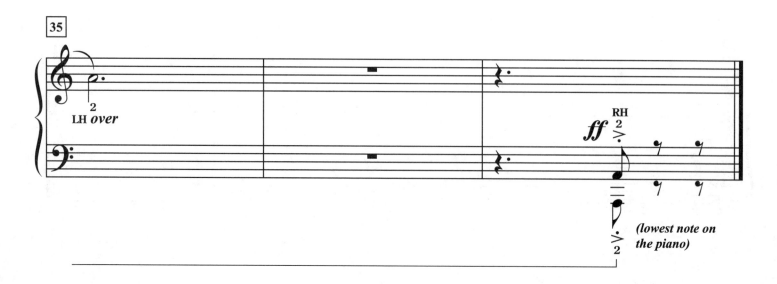

(lowest note on
the piano)

Primo

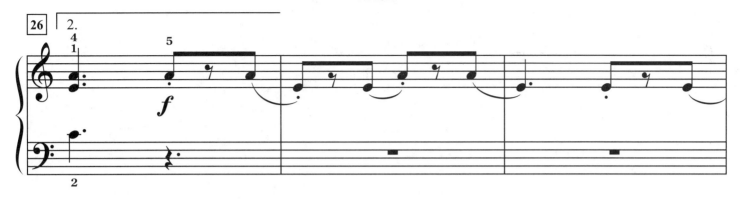

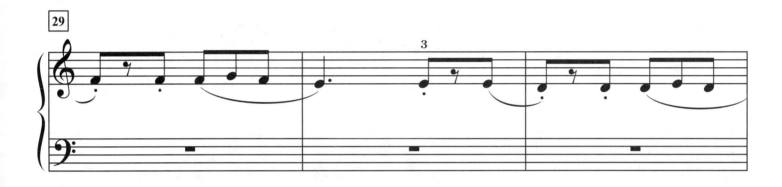

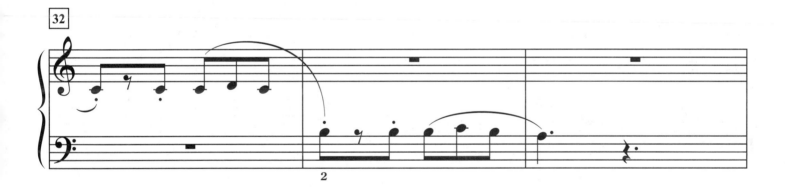

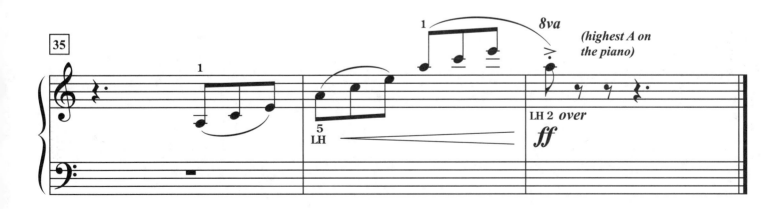

Polovetsian Dance

(from the opera *Prince Igor*)

Secondo

Alexander Borodin
Arranged by Carol Matz

Polovetsian Dance

(from the opera *Prince Igor*)

Primo

Alexander Borodin
Arranged by Carol Matz

Flowing
Play both hands one octave higher

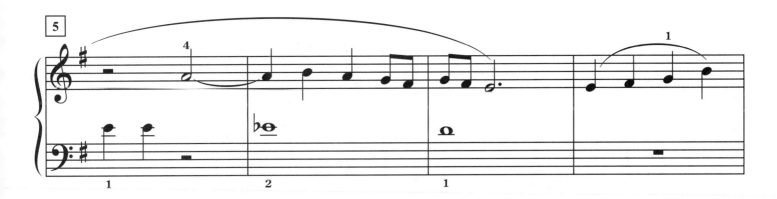

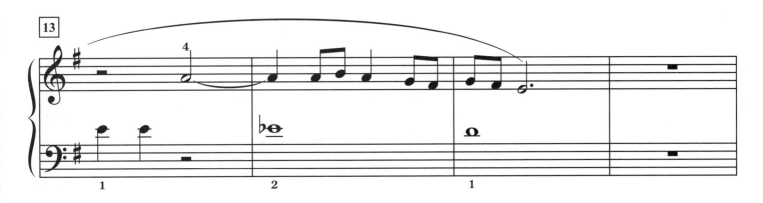

Secondo

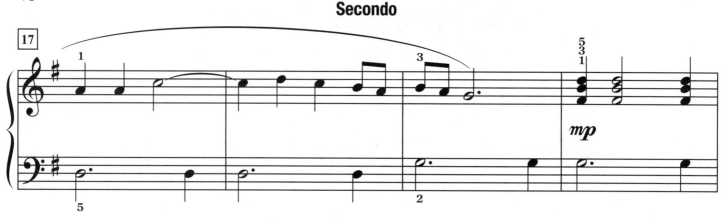

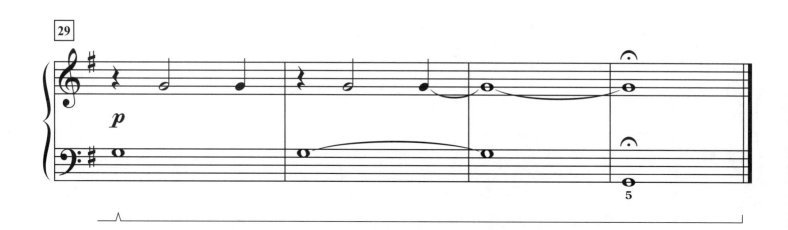

Primo

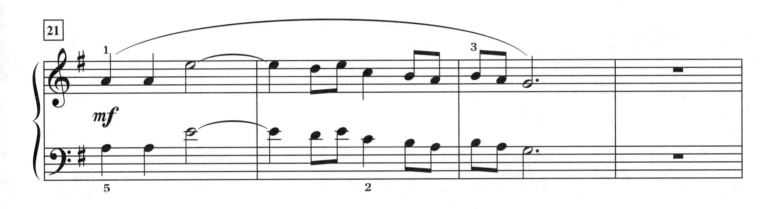

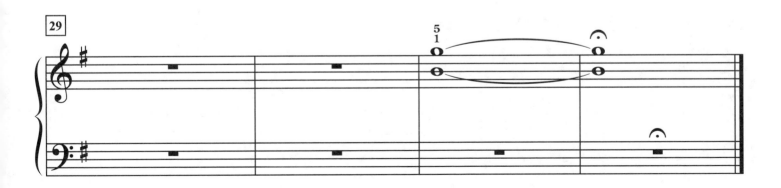

Washington Post March

Secondo

John Philip Sousa
Arranged by Carol Matz

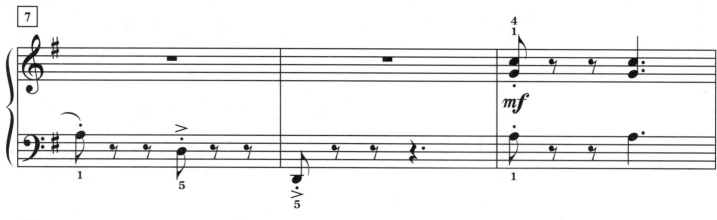

Washington Post March

Primo

John Philip Sousa
Arranged by Carol Matz

Moderately fast

Play both hands one octave higher

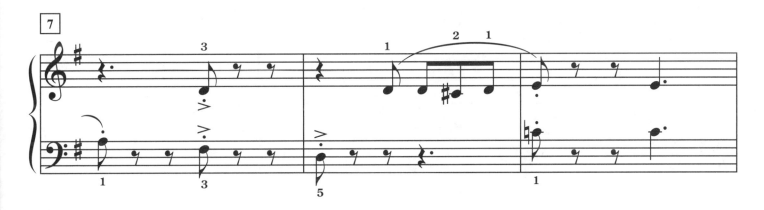

Secondo

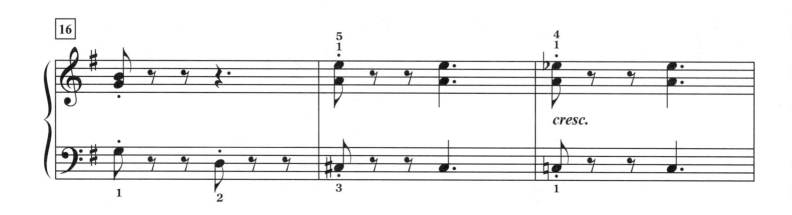

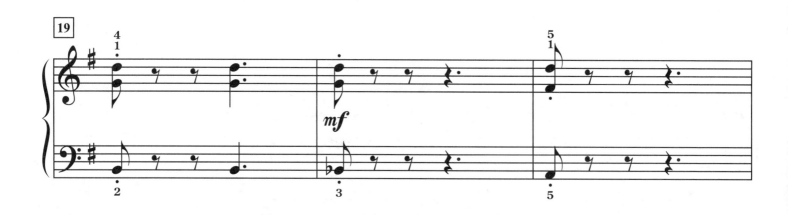

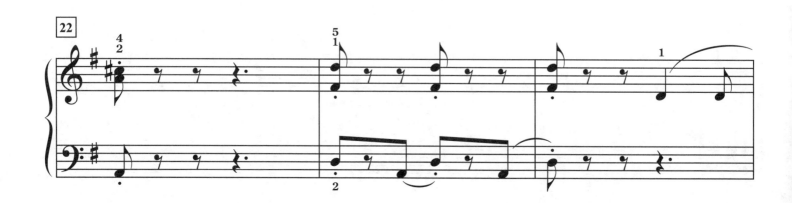

Primo

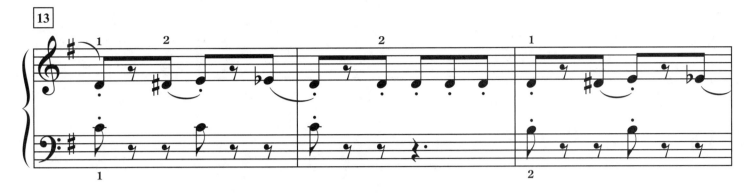

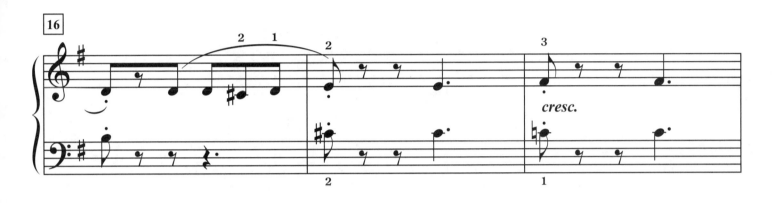

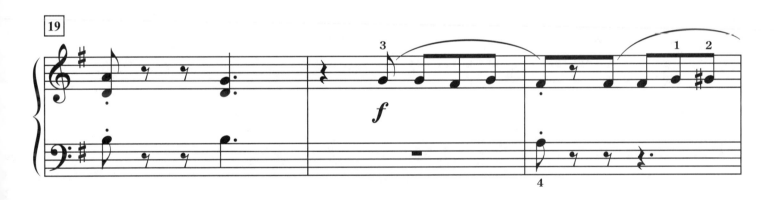

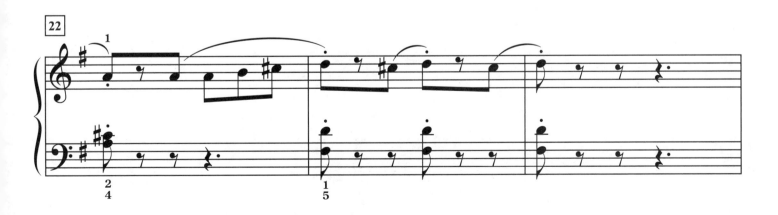

Secondo

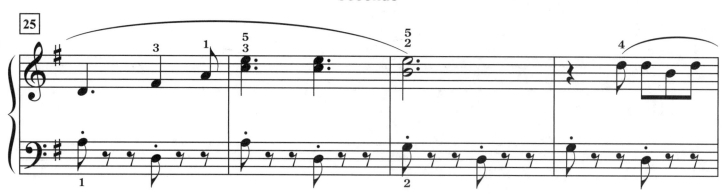

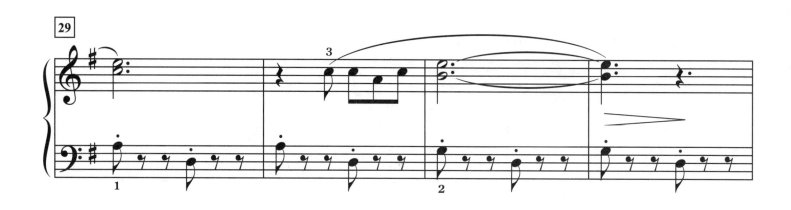

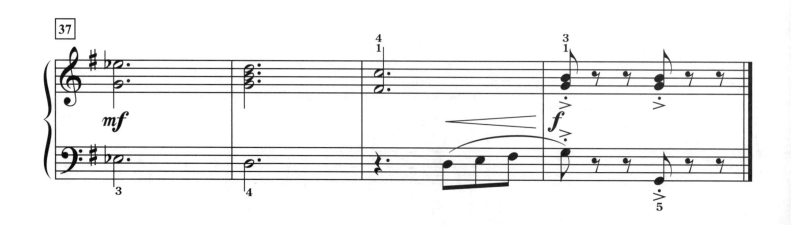

Primo

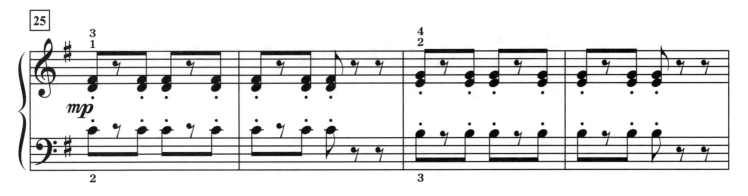

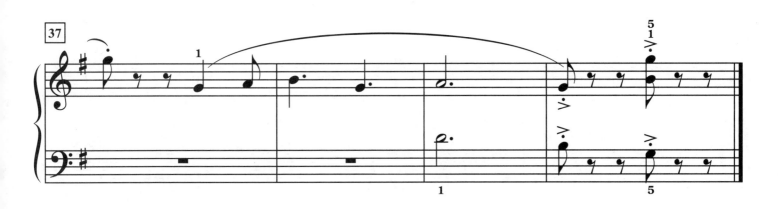

Theme from

Piano Concerto in A Minor

(First Movement)

Secondo

Edvard Grieg
Arranged by Carol Matz

Moderately

Play both hands one octave lower

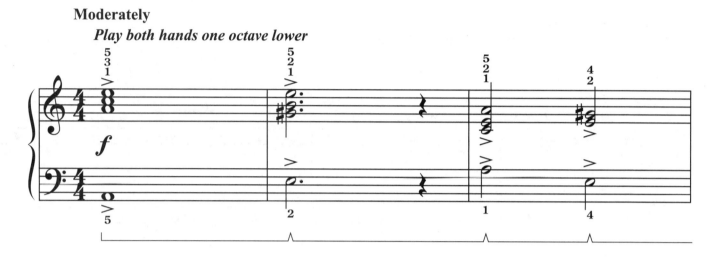

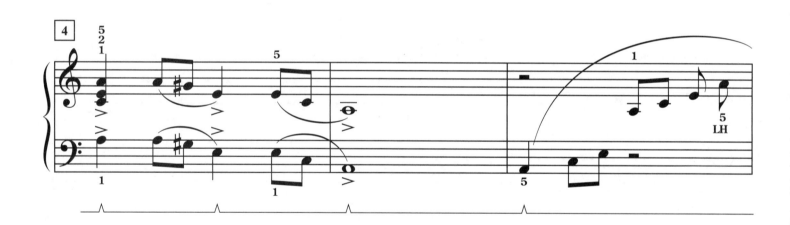

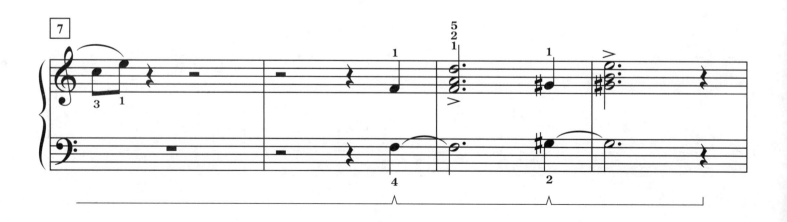

Theme from

Piano Concerto in A Minor

(First Movement)

Primo

Edvard Grieg
Arranged by Carol Matz

Moderately
Play both hands one octave higher

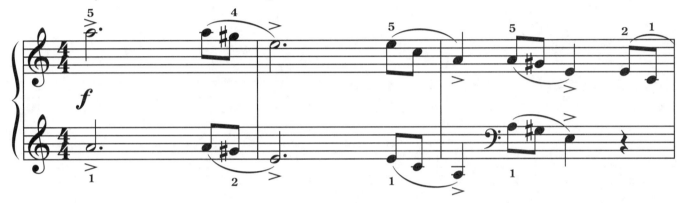

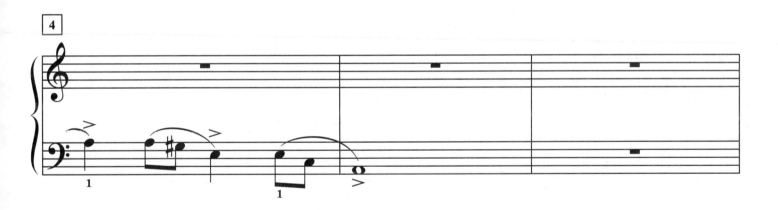

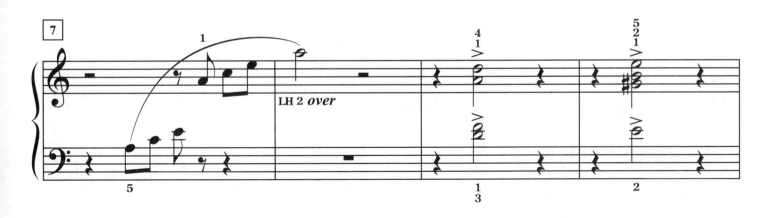

Secondo

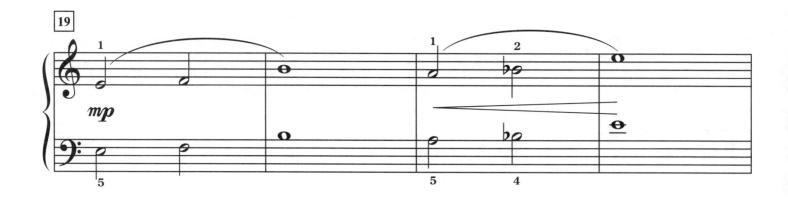

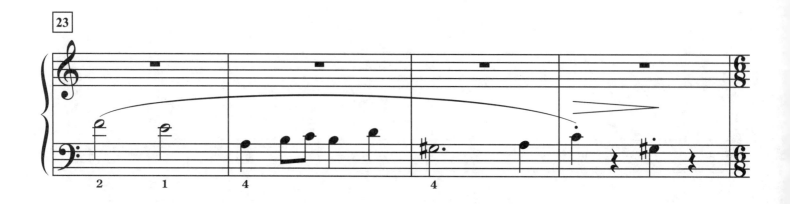

Primo

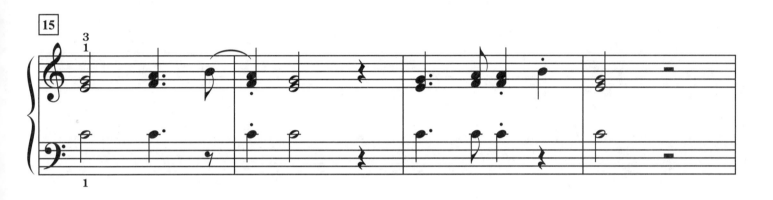

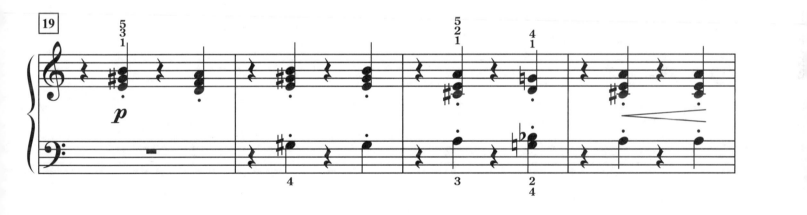

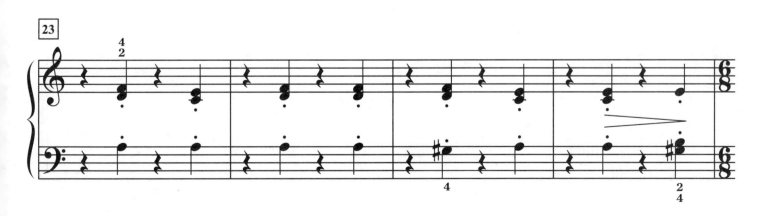

Secondo

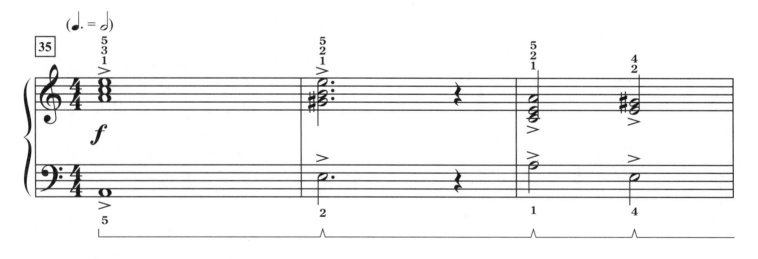

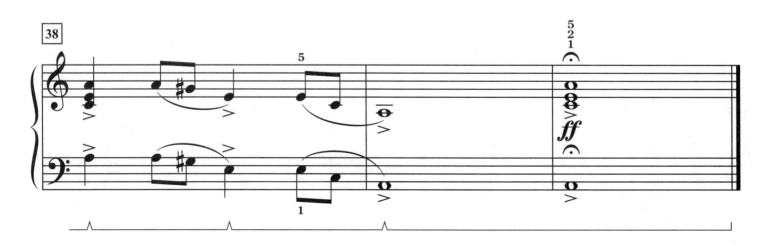

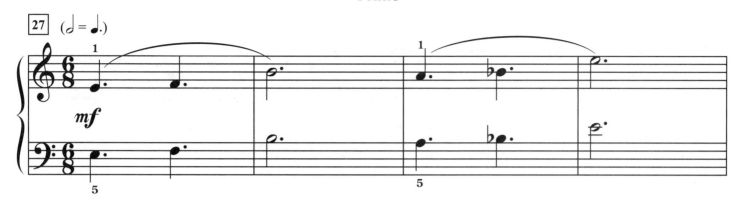

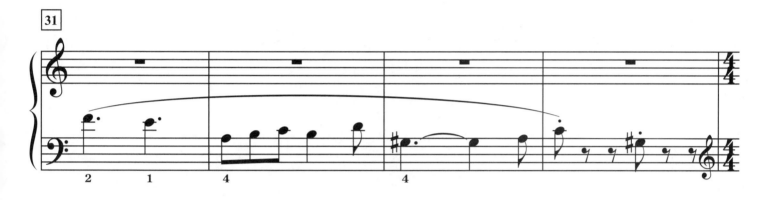

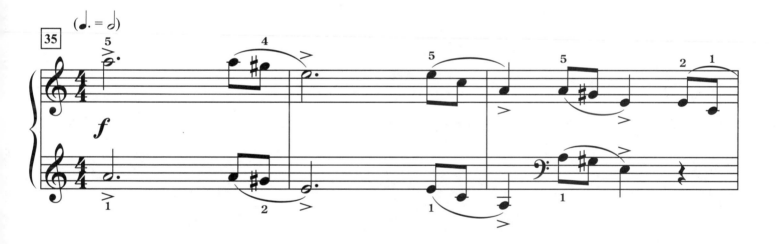